CW01003827

OCH AYE *the* G'NU

Five Mile, an imprint of
Bonnier Publishing Australia
Level 6, 534 Church Street,
Richmond, Victoria 3121

www.fivemile.com.au

First published 2017
Printed in China 5 4 3 2 1

Produced by Paul Field. Early Childhood Advisors: Kathleen Warren EdD,
MA (Hons) LASA, FTCL and Anthony Field, AM, DipEd, HonDUniv,
HonLittD. Audio Engineer: Jeff McCormack. Production Manager:
Ivy Gaymer. Musicians and Performers: Jimmy Barnes (poetry reading),
Jackie Barnes (percussion, sound effects and vocals), Jeff Fatt (piano,
accordion and animal noises), additional noises by Paul and Murray.
Nourishment by Jane Barnes.

The RECORDED POEMS of

OCH AYE *the*
G'NU

as written and told by
JIMMY BARNES

FIVE
MILE

The Wiggles
PRODUCTION

*T*his book belongs to:

....

This is for all the little ones out there.

*Live life and dream of a world
where every child can be happy.*

You are our future.

And for all my grandchildren:

I love you all so much.

Letter from Jimmy

Hello friends, old and G'nu!

Welcome to the wonderful world of Och Aye the G'Nu and his best friend Kangaroo. Two happy young beasts who live in the Glasgow Zoo. I hope that they can take you along with them on their adventures as they laugh and play together. Best friends for life.

Best wishes,

The Recorded Poems of Och Aye the G'Nu

CONTENTS

Och Aye
the G'Nu

Och Aye the G'Nu

*T*hough g'nus come from Africa,
he lived in a zoo.

In a land that was wet
and a bitter wind blew.

And the snow and the bagpipes
were all that he knew.

And he went by the name
of young Och Aye the G'Nu.

*N*ow Och Aye the G'Nu
had a voice that cut through.

He was happy and lived
with his friend Kangaroo.

When he danced and he sang
with a hullabaloo.

All the animals cheered
for young Och Aye the G'Nu.

He would tell them to bark,
he would tell them to moo.

As the children rowed by
in a big green canoe.

He would jump in the air
when they came into view.

And the word spread around
about Och Aye the G'Nu.

Well, they came from afar –
all the way from Peru.

And they were happy to wait,
they were happy to queue.

All their faces lit up
and the sky seemed so blue.

When they stood and they gazed
at young Och Aye the G'Nu.

Every day there were more
and the crowds grew and grew.

He would think of new tricks
that he tried to outdo.

Instead of four legs
he could stand up on two.

And the children cheered loudly
YIPPEE!
for Och Aye the G'Nu.

The Queen and the Prince
and the Grand Great Wazoo.

Came to visit with Sheiks
and a Caliph or two.

They could look but not touch,
that was strictly taboo.

They all curtseyed and bowed low
to Och Aye the G'Nu.

He would march up and down
with the Scottish Tattoo.

So they made him a kilt
in a tartan or two.

And the elephant trumpeted
songs that he knew.

An extraordinary beast
was young Och Aye the G'Nu.

They brought hay for the horse,
for the panda bamboo.

For the tigers and lions
they brought Mulligan stew.

Fruit for the bats,
all their wishes came true.

They all ate like kings
'cause of Och Aye the G'Nu.

As you're falling asleep
maybe dreams can come true.

Keep on travelling north
'til he comes into view.

He's a handsome young calf,
he's a wildebeest, too.

But in Scotland they call him
young Och Aye the G'Nu.

THE END

Och Aye
and
Kangaroo

Och Aye and Kangaroo

*E*very wildebeest
needs a good friend who is true.

A shoulder to cry on
'cause that's what friends do.

One who knows when to laugh
and a listener, too.

That someone is Kanga
for Och Aye the G'Nu.

*O*ch Aye met dear Kanga
the first time he flew.

On a flight that was headed
to places anew.

It was all very strange
and it scared Kangaroo.

And his paw held the hoof
of young Och Aye the G'Nu.

From that day they were friends
and the bond grew and grew.

They stood close together
that day in the zoo.

And the Glasgow keepers
then very well knew.

Those friends needed to be
in a room made for two.

People thought it was strange
to see two stuck like glue.

When one of them moved,
the other did, too.

They stayed side by side,
they were friends through and through.

The young G'Nu, Och Aye
and his friend Kangaroo.

If Kanga was sad,

OH!

Och Aye knew what to do.

He'd hop around the yard
and say, 'I'm just like you!'

He would talk like the old friends
that Kangaroo knew.

The koala, the dingo
and platypus, too.

When Och Aye felt sad
OH!
as indeed we all do.

Then the cheering up task
was done by Kangaroo.

Och Aye missed his herd,
he missed Africa, too.

They sang African songs
and the lions joined in, too.
ROAR!

Kangaroo was his friend
and everyone knew.

That playing with one
would mean playing with two.

They shared water and food
and they shared blankets, too.

They shared a great love,
did that Kanga and G'Nu.

When you go to Scotland,
make sure that you do.

Take a trip just to see
what's at Glasgow Zoo.

You might see those friends
that could not break in two.

I mean Och Aye the G'Nu
and his friend Kangaroo.

THE END

POEM G'NUMBER 3

The G'Nu's
Sea Cruise

The G'Nu's Sea Cruise

'*I*'ve been dreaming of a sea cruise,'
thought Och Aye the happy G'Nu.

We'll sail into the deep,
across the oceans blue.

Across the waves we'll splish and splash
in a boat built just for two.

We'll see the world together
me and my friend Kangaroo.

We'll set sail in the morning,
best bid all our friends adieu.

We'll tie some ropes and hoist the sails
'cause that's what sailors do.

I couldn't do it all alone,
every captain needs a crew.
AHOY!

And no one could be better
than my best friend Kangaroo.

We'll be leaving from G'Northampton
on our way by half-past two.

And try to reach G'Newfoundland
before the day is through.

Around the horn, across the straits,
navigating true.

Exploring as we go along,
Och Aye and Kangaroo.

The dolphins swim and lead the way
– the flying fish do, too.

They duck and dive across the waves
that roll and roll on through.

We'll follow them by day and night,
oh, what a lovely cruise!

The sun, the sea, the fish, the breeze,
Och Aye and Kangaroo.

We might just hear a whale sing
with a voice so clear and true.

If we listen as he calls his friends,
'come swimming with me, too!'

The song is soft, the singing sweet,
so how could they refuse?

I think we'll go along with them,
my dear friend Kangaroo.

I know there's nothing quite as good
as a summer-long sea cruise.

But hooves and paws need solid ground
and not the oceans blue.

We'd have to make a lot of stops
to find some grass to chew.

So best we don't stray far from land,
old jumping Kangaroo.

$\mathcal{M}$aybe we can see the sea
from right here in the zoo.

If we look across the city
below the sky, there in the view.

We wouldn't have to get so wet
or tell our friends the news.

That we were leaving in the morning
on a windy, wet sea cruise.

So if you go to Scotland
they're still waiting there for you.

Dreaming of a long sea voyage
that they will never do.

Come right through the big front gate,
right there in Glasgow Zoo.

And see if you can find your friends,
HELLO!
Och Aye and Kangaroo.

The G'Nu's
New Shoes

The G'Nu's New Shoes

A very fine wildebeest
lived in a zoo.

In a land full of castles
and flags that were blue.

He had a heart that was brave
and a heart that was true.

With his beard oh so red,
he was Och Aye the G'Nu.

The sun had been smiling
on Och Aye the G'Nu.

But the summer was leaving
and saying, 'adieu'.

Now the winter was coming
and he needed shoes.

And you need four – not two –
to shoe Och Aye the G'Nu.

*I*n his kilt he was handsome,
his fame grew and grew.

But where he'd find shoes,
he just hadn't a clue.

So he asked everyone,
then he heard from a shrew.

'Time to go to the shop,'
it told Och Aye the G'Nu.

$\mathcal{H}$e went down the high street,
not far from the zoo.

And he looked in the windows –
but shoe shops were few.

Then he laughed out aloud
as they came into view.

A fine pair of boots
fit for Och Aye the G'Nu.

*H*e squeezed and he groaned
and he let out a 'phew'.

'Til he found himself boots
he could fit right into.

They made him look taller
than a goat or a ewe.

Then he strutted around
canny Och Aye the G'Nu.

*H*e clipped and he clopped,
and he blew his kazoo.

He jumped and he kicked
as you do in kung fu.

When he danced and he sang
every animal knew.

How happy his shoes made him,
Och Aye the G'Nu.

The elephant shouted out,
'I want some, too!'

And the peacock he wanted a pair –
powder blue.

The crocodile said,
'I need shoes to wear, too!'

He had started a trend now
had Och Aye the G'Nu.

Well, the zoo keeper laughed,

HA, HA, HA, HA!

'I'll see what I can do.'

And he looked in the papers
to see who made shoes.

Then he saw there were sales
and he read the reviews.

And they all went out shopping
with Och Aye the G'Nu.

'Let's stop for some lunch,

MMMMM!

we can have Irish stew!'

'Not for me,' said the cow,
'but some grass I could chew.'

So they walked and they slid
and some of them flew.

In a conga line following
Och Aye the G'Nu.

$\mathcal{N}$ow I tell you no lies
all the story is true.

When the snow starts to fall
if you come to the zoo.

All the animals there
will be wearing their shoes.

And dancing along
with old Och Aye the G'Nu.

THE END

POEM G'NUMBER 5

Och Aye
Gets the Flu

Och Aye Gets the Flu

We all know in the cold
we must always wear shoes.

But it's hard if you've hooves
just like horses or g'nus.

They feel fine for a time,
but to tell you what's true.

He likes his four feet
does old Och Aye the G'Nu.

*T*he snow felt so cold
and deliciously new.

He ran out of his house
and he kicked off his shoes.

And he jumped and he skipped
and he danced the day through.

Only then he could see
that his hooves had turned blue.

*B*ut he played on for hours,
then let out an

AAAACHOO!

And he felt hot and sickly
so he asked Kangaroo,

'What could make my nose run
and my eyes bright red, too?'

He said, 'You've caught a cold,
poor old Och Aye the G'Nu.'

Kanga made a hot drink
full of herbs boiled and brewed.

Then he added some lemons
that the snake squeezed to juice.

'The bees gave me honey
so the best thing to do.

Is to drink it right down,
then to bed, you sweet G'Nu.'

'And I've knitted a blanket
with some wool from the ewes.

They gave fleece off their backs,'
declared Kangaroo.

'Flocks of birds with their beaks
sewed your name on it, too.

To help fight off the cold,
just for Och Aye the G'Nu.'

*H*e coughed and he groaned
and he sneezed, 'achoo!'
whispering, 'phew!'

'I don't like feeling ill,'
he told his friend Kangaroo.

'Well, you must stay in bed,
there's nothin' else you can do!

And cold will soon pass,
my dear Och Aye the G'Nu.'

*T*he next day Och Aye woke
and he yelled out,

'YAHOO!'

Not a trace of that cold,
he felt great! Good as new!

So to thank his good friends
he ran all round the zoo.

And he gathered up flowers
for his friend Kangaroo.

So remember that everyone,
and that means you, too.

Can come down with a cold
or could even get the flu.

So best keep warm and dry
as your mother tells you.

Or you might end up sick
like poor Och Aye the G'Nu.

THE END

Och Aye Sings the Blues

Och Aye Sings the Blues

*T*he wind was blowing cold,
the sky was grey, not blue.

The bears slept in their caves
dreaming the winter through.

The wild dogs had their woolly coats
and everybody knew.

That winter was upon them,
except for young Och Aye the G'Nu.

*H*e loved the sunshine on his back
as warm as cheese fondue.

Where he came from it was always warm,
the cold wind never blew.

It made him feel a wee bit sad,
so all that he could do.

Was raise his voice up to the sky
and Och Aye sang the blues.

*H*is voice it trembled as he sang
a song heartfelt and true.

He touched each beast that heard him sing
from mouse to cockatoo.

The panda swayed and sang along
while eating his bamboo.

And each and every heart felt sad
when Och Aye sang the blues.

*H*e wailed and screamed
then whispered low,

SHHH!

sang every note he knew.

The strangest thing then happened –
he started dancing, too!

He jumped so high into the air,
he touched the sky! He flew!

It really was a sight to see
when Och Aye sang the blues.

*T*he keepers thought he sounded sick

OH!

and hoped he would pull through.

The more he sang and danced he felt
the better his voice grew.

He brayed and honked
and squeaked and squawked
through every song he knew.

It sounded like a symphony
when Och Aye sang the blues.

*T*hen every beast that shared the zoo
joined in the singing, too.

A penguin honked, a monkey squealed
and hopped with Kangaroo.

They kept the beat for all to sing
with noises pure and true.

They raised their voices loud and clear
when Och Aye sang the blues.

*T*he antelopes jumped,
the elephant bumped,
the zebras marched in twos.

The snake let out the loudest hiss,
the warthog wrote reviews.

UNBELIEVABLE!

The tiger spread the word around

ROAR!

so that everybody knew.

It was like a party going on
when Och Aye sang the blues.

They sang all night, 'a-ha'
'til morning light, 'a-ha'
and then the sound subdued.

'Twas time to sleep, shhh!
and rest their feet
and rest their voices, too.

AHH!

When they opened up gates next day
and let all the people through.

A massive crowd soon gathered round
HOORAY!
while Och Aye sang the blues.

*S*o when you come to Glasgow
take some time to see the zoo.

And if you come in winter time,
your dreams just might come true.

So when it's cold, come past the chimps
and past the caribou.

And join the crowds who clap and cheer
HOORAY!
when Och Aye sings the blues.

THE END

Happy Birthday G'Nu

Happy Birthday G'Nu

'*T*here's a party tonight!'
said the sweet Kangaroo.

'It's a secret,
SHHH!
So don't tell young Och Aye the G'Nu.

It's his birthday today,
yes, today he turns two!

It's a great big
SURPRISE!
And G'Nu hasn't a clue.'

'*H*e thinks we don't know
or he thinks we forgot.

He told no one last year,
so we started a plot.

We'll
SURPRISE!
Och Aye this time.

Keep it under our hats,
SHHH!

But everyone's comin',
yes, even the bats.'

'There'll be cordial and candy
and candles and cake.

MMMMM!

The swans will be swimming
as they glide 'cross the lake.

We'll have jelly and ice cream
and big red balloons.

We can bounce and blow bubbles
with baby baboons.'

'The snake can throw streamers,
the zebra will jump.

Over fences for fun
and his hooves will go thump!

The flamingos will dance
and the brolgas will sway.

The hippos will roar,
ROAR, HIP-HIP HOORAY!'

'Yes, tonight there's a party
in old Glasgow Zoo.

And we're goin' to sing
HAPPY BIRTHDAY G'NU!'

THE END